D1710279

# ZOMBIE ANIMALS
## PARASITES TAKE CONTROL!

# ZOMBIE CRABS

BY JOLENE ALESSI

Gareth Stevens
PUBLISHING

Please visit our website, www.garethstevens.com. For a free color catalog of all our high-quality books, call toll free 1-800-542-2595 or fax 1-877-542-2596.

**Library of Congress Cataloging-in-Publication Data**

Alessi, Jolene.
Zombie crabs / by Jolene Alessi.
p. cm. — (Zombie animals: parasites take control!)
Includes index.
ISBN 978-1-4824-2836-0 (pbk.)
ISBN 978-1-4824-2837-7 (6 pack)
ISBN 978-1-4824-2838-4 (library binding)
1. Parasites — Juvenile literature. 2. Host-parasite relationships — Juvenile literature. 3. Crabs — Juvenile literature. I. Title.
QL757.A447 2016
578.6'5—d23

First Edition

Published in 2016 by
**Gareth Stevens Publishing**
111 East 14th Street, Suite 349
New York, NY 10003

Copyright © 2016 Gareth Stevens Publishing

Designer: Nicholas Domiano and Laura Bowen
Editor: Kristen Rajczak

Photo credits: Cover, pp. 1 (crab), 21 (middle) Hans Hillewaert/Wikimedia Commons; cover, p.1 (ocean floor) Dudarev Mikhail/Shutterstock.com; p. 5 MyLoupe/Universal Images Group/Getty Images; p. 7 (main) © iStockphoto.com/yxowert; p. 7 (inset) Robert F. Sisson/National Geographic/Getty Images; p. 9 Gdr/Wikimedia Commons; pp. 11, 21 (bottom) Auguste Le Roux/Wikimedia Commons; p. 13 (main) BSIP/Universal Images Group/Getty Images; p. 13 (inset) Mary Hollinger/NOAA Picture Library/Wikimedia Commons; p. 15 Education Images/Universal Images Group/Getty Images; p. 17 Auscape/Universal Images Group/Getty Images; p. 19 George Chernilevsky/Wikimedia Commons; p. 21 (top) Paul Kay/Oxford Scientific/Getty Images.

Printed in the United States of America

CPSIA compliance information: Batch #CS15GS: For further information contact Gareth Stevens, New York, New York at 1-800-542-2595.

# CONTENTS

Words in the glossary appear in **bold** type the first time they are used in the text.

# BAD BARNACLES

The European green crab isn't easy to kill. It has claws that can turn to attack predators behind it. This ocean dweller can live in freshwater for a short time and even live *out* of water for about a week! The green crab eats just about everything, too, including clams and small lobsters.

However, barnacles called *Sacculina carcini* can harm the green crab. *S. carcini* takes over a crab's body to grow and **reproduce**. The crab becomes a zombie!

## TAKE-OVER TRUTHS

*S. CARCINI* IS ONE OF ABOUT 230 SPECIES, OR KINDS, OF BARNACLES IN THE ANIMAL GROUP RHIZOCEPHALA (RY-ZOH-**SEH**-FUH-LUH). THEY'RE ALL **PARASITES**!

Green crabs are found on coasts all over the world, though they're native to coasts of Europe and North Africa.

# HUNTING FOR A HOME

S. carcini larvae look much like the larvae of other kinds of barnacles. They're **microscopic** and teardrop shaped. Each larva swims along in the ocean on its own, **molting** several times as it grows. It becomes either male or female.

Most barnacle larvae find a rock or other hard surface to stick to. They grow a shell and live out their adulthood happily taking their food from the water around them. S. carcini larvae look for a crab instead!

## TAKE-OVER TRUTHS

S. CARCINI'S MAIN **HOST** IS THE GREEN CRAB. HOWEVER, IT ALSO COMMONLY **INFECTS** SWIMMING CRABS IN THE ANIMAL GROUP PORTUNIDAE.

S. CARCINI LARVA

Unlike these adult barnacles, *S. carcini*'s larvae would never settle on a rock or on the bottom of a boat. They need a host!

# TAKING ROOT

Once a female larva lands on a crab, she looks for a place where the crab's **exoskeleton** is thinner and weaker. She uses a sharp, needlelike body part to push a hole into the crab. Then, she leaves behind most of her body and pushes her soft inner body into the crab.

The larva now looks like a tiny, fat worm—but not for long! *S. carcini* begins to grow throughout the crab's body. It feeds on the **nutrients** the crab takes in.

## TAKE-OVER TRUTHS

WHAT IS THE CRAB DOING WHILE THE PARASITE ENTERS ITS BODY? NOTHING! *S. CARCINI* SHUTS DOWN THE PARTS OF THE CRAB'S BODY THAT ATTACK **INVADERS**.

The growth of *S. carcini* inside a crab's body can be compared to how a plant's roots grow underground.

# OUT OF THE BODY

The "roots" *S. carcini* has grown inside the crab are called the interna. Once they're fully grown, *S. carcini* begins to grow outside of the crab's body. The crab molts a final time, making room for a sac-like reproductive **organ** that sticks out of its **abdomen**.

By the time this organ appears, the crab is fully under the parasite's control. The crab will stop molting. It does eat a lot, but all the energy from the food goes to the parasite.

## TAKE-OVER TRUTHS

THE REPRODUCTIVE ORGAN OF *S. CARCINI* IS CALLED THE EXTERNA.

This image clearly shows the externa growing out of the abdomen of a crab.

# ZOMBIE DAD

*S. carcini* grows its externa right where female crabs carry their egg pouch—on the abdomen. But what if the parasite has infected a male crab?

*S. carcini* makes the male crab think it's female! The parasite uses **chemicals** to destroy the crab's male reproductive parts. What's more, it makes the male crab's body look more like a female crab's body by widening the abdomen. The male crab starts to act like a female ready to care for her eggs.

## TAKE-OVER TRUTHS

ONE CRAB COULD BE HOME TO MORE THAN ONE *S. CARCINI* PARASITE!

MALE

FEMALE

Male and female crabs have different-shaped bodies. *S. carcini* needs a male's abdomen to be wider like the female's!

13

# A BIG ARRIVAL

The male larvae of *S. carcini* are also on the lookout for crabs. But they want to find one that's already been infected with female *S. carcini*. Chemicals given off by the externa draw the male larvae to the right crabs.

A male larva needs to find a tiny hole on the outside of the externa. Like the female larva when infecting the crab, the male larva leaves behind most of its body to fit into it. Now, *S. carcini* has everything it needs to reproduce!

## TAKE-OVER TRUTHS

THERE'S ROOM FOR TWO MALE LARVAE TO **FERTILIZE** THE EGGS IN THE EXTERNA AT ONE TIME. THIS ALLOWS FOR *THE* GREATEST AMOUNT OF REPRODUCTION!

The only way *S. carcini* can reproduce to create other zombie crabs is by drawing in male larvae.

# THE ZOMBIE LIFE

The zombie crab lives only for the parasite now. Under normal conditions, crabs may lose a claw when trying to escape a predator and be able to regrow it. When infected with this parasite, a crab can no longer do so.

The crab cares for *S. carcini*'s externa just as a female crab cares for its egg pouch. It removes anything that grows on the externa. Male crabs would never do this if they weren't infected with *S. carcini*!

## TAKE-OVER TRUTHS

*S. CARCINI* HAS NO NATURAL PREDATORS OF ITS OWN WHEN IT LIVES INSIDE THE CRAB. HOWEVER, ITS PREDATORS ARE WHATEVER THE CRAB'S PREDATORS ARE!

This female crab has a real pouch full of eggs. Look back at the image on page 11. The reproductive organ grown by *S. carcini* looks very similar!

# THE FINAL STEP

Under the parasite's control, the zombie crab believes it's carrying its own eggs. So, when *S. carcini* larvae are ready to hatch, or come out, the crab acts just as it would when its own larvae are about to hatch.

The crab first climbs to a place higher in the water where the current moves quickly. Then, it bobs around, forcing the larvae out of the externa. The crab waves its claws around to help them swim away.

## TAKE-OVER TRUTHS

*S. CARCINI* CAN PRODUCE THOUSANDS OF NEW LARVAE EVERY FEW WEEKS.

Under the control of *S. carcini*, a crab thinks it's spreading its own larvae in the ocean. Really, it's helping spread a parasite to other crabs!

# INFECTING ON PURPOSE?

The European green crab is an invasive species. In order to control its population, some scientists have suggested infecting them with *S. carcini*. However, while the parasite's favorite host is the green crab, it will also infect other crabs. That means putting it in the water near green crabs could also hurt native crab populations.

*S. carcini* is just one of millions of parasites on Earth. But it's also one of only a few that can make a zombie of its host!

## TAKE-OVER TRUTHS

AN INVASIVE SPECIES IS A KIND OF ANIMAL THAT'S NOT NATIVE TO AN AREA AND CAUSES HARM TO ITS NEW HOME.

# THE MAKING OF A ZOMBIE CRAB

female *S. carcini* larva enters a crab through a tiny hole in the exoskeleton

the interna grows throughout the crab's body

if the crab is male, *S. carcini* makes chemicals to make it act and look female

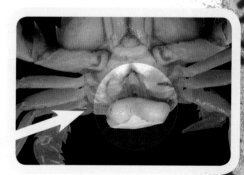

the externa grows on the crab's abdomen

male larva fertilizes *S. carcini*'s eggs

the crab cares for and hatches the parasite's eggs

# GLOSSARY

**abdomen:** the part of an animal's body that contains the stomach

**chemical:** matter that can be mixed with other matter to cause changes

**exoskeleton:** the hard outer covering of an animal's body

**fertilize:** to add male cells to a female's eggs to make babies

**host:** the animal on or in which a parasite lives

**infect:** to spread something harmful inside the body

**invader:** something or someone that arrives with the goal of causing harm

**microscopic:** very small

**molt:** to leave behind an outer covering that has become too small

**nutrient:** something a living thing needs to grow and stay alive

**organ:** a part inside an animal's body

**parasite:** a living thing that lives in, on, or with another living thing and often causes it harm

**reproduce:** to create another creature like oneself

# FOR MORE INFORMATION

## BOOKS

Larson, Kirsten. *Zombies in Nature*. Mankato, MN: Amicus, 2016.

West, David. *Tide Pool Animals*. Mankato, MN: Smart Apple Media, 2014.

## WEBSITES

**Crab Facts for Kids**
*animalstime.com/crab-facts-kids-top-10-crab-facts-for-kids/*
Learn about all different kinds of crabs!

**Rhizocephala: The Extraordinary Life Cycle of a Parasitic Barnacle**
*vimeo.com/38529527*
This simple video explains the life cycle of Rhizocephala and their parasitic relationship with crabs.

# INDEX